This edition published in 1993 by Rainbow Books,
Elsley House, 24-30 Great Titchfield Street, London W1P 7AD

First published in 1989 by Kingfisher Books Ltd in the Stories *Farm Animal Stories*

10 9 8 7 6 5 4 3 2 1

© Grisewood & Dempsey Ltd 1989

ISBN 1 85698 037 5

Printed in Italy

OLD MACDONALD'S FARM

# THE PONY

By Angela Royston

Illustrated by Bob Bampton

RAINBOW
·BOOKS·

Early one spring morning the little foal is born. He struggles to stand but falls down. He tries again and again until he can balance on his long, wobbly legs. The mare licks and nibbles him. He gives a little cry and his mother answers with a soft neigh.

He starts to search for her udder. He gently pushes at her belly and nudges his way along her body. He accidentally bumps her udder and is surprised by the taste of the warm milk that flows over his face. Then he finds her teat and sucks until he is full.

At first the foal sleeps and feeds most of the time.
But after a few days his legs become stronger. Soon
he is happily running and playing around his
mother. He trots and canters and jumps into the air.

One day his mother rolls over onto her back with her legs in the air. She does this because her skin is itchy but the little foal is so excited that he snorts, lifts his tail and jumps round her.

At night the mare and her foal are led into a stable. The mare's coat is brushed and her mane is combed. The foal is brushed too and they both have their feet cleaned with a hoof pick. The foal becomes restless and is pleased when grooming is over. His mother nuzzles him and they lie down to sleep.

By the time the foal is a few months old he is happy to wander farther from his mother, while he nibbles the fresh summer grass. He likes to watch the other ponies with their riders in the next paddock.

Sometimes people come to the gate of their field. His
mother goes over to be stroked and he follows her.
The foal likes being patted. He is very curious. He
sees an interesting hat and tries to lick it.

As the foal eats more grass he drinks less of his mother's milk. When he is six months old his mother is taken from him. He looks for her and neighs loudly but he cannot see her anywhere.

That afternoon a young horse is put into the field with him. She comes to greet the foal. At first he is frightened and puts his ears back, but after a while he is glad the horse is there.

The foal and the horse are soon good friends. They graze together, rest together and nibble each other's coats. One day they are grazing under an apple tree when two apples fall from the tree onto the foal's back. The foal is startled.

He whinnies, throws up his head and gallops away. The horse follows him. They circle the field and then return to the tree. The horse finds a fallen apple and crunches it down eagerly. The foal picks up a bit of it and enjoys its sweet taste.

One morning all the horses and ponies are kept in their stables. The blacksmith is coming to check their feet. The foal is now a young pony and is called a colt. He watches as the blacksmith hammers new shoes onto the horses' feet.

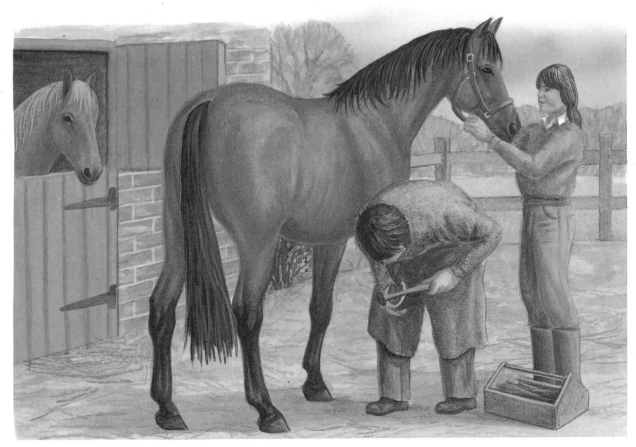

The colt is not ready for shoes yet but the
blacksmith lifts his feet one by one and trims off
some of his hard hoof. He can hardly feel it.

The colt is nearly four years old and is ready to be trained to take a rider. He is already used to wearing a head collar, but now he learns to 'halt' and to 'walk on' when he is told.

After a few days a long rein is attached to his collar and the colt walks in a wide circle around his trainer. The colt enjoys his training. He is stroked and given some carrot when he has done well. After a few weeks he can go round without the rein, walking, trotting, cantering and halting.

Over the next few months the young pony learns to wear a bridle around his head and gets used to the feel of the bit in his mouth. He has a saddle put on his back and, later, someone lies across it so that he can get used to her weight. His trainer talks to him all the time to keep him calm.

At last the young pony is ready to take his first rider on his back. Soon he will be able to join the other ponies in the riding stables.

## More About Ponies

The pony in this story is a New Forest pony. Some of these ponies live wild in the New Forest in in southern Britain, but, like the Exmoor pony, many are bred on special farms called stud farms.

Exmoor

Falabella

Iceland

Horses and ponies are measured in hands from the ground to the top of the withers. A hand is 10 centimetres, that is about as wide as an adult's hand. All ponies are less than 14.2 hands high. The smallest ponies are the Falabella ponies which may be only 4 hands high and are too small to ride. Ponies are strong and hardy. Iceland ponies have been used as working ponies ever since the Vikings.

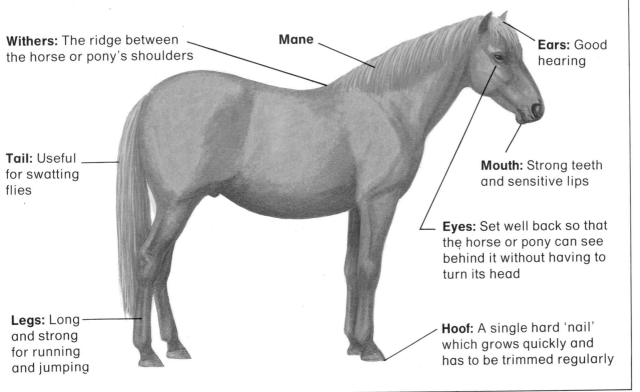

**Withers:** The ridge between the horse or pony's shoulders

**Mane**

**Ears:** Good hearing

**Tail:** Useful for swatting flies

**Mouth:** Strong teeth and sensitive lips

**Eyes:** Set well back so that the horse or pony can see behind it without having to turn its head

**Legs:** Long and strong for running and jumping

**Hoof:** A single hard 'nail' which grows quickly and has to be trimmed regularly